I0465991

Bitcoin and Crypto Scams

How to avoid bitcoin and cryptocurrency scams

ISBN: 9781792671807

Zach Abraham

Table of Contents

Introduction

If you haven't been living under a rock for the past 5 years, chances are you have probably heard of the words Bitcoin or crypto currency. Bitcoin and cryptocurrency are trending buzzwords that have taken the world by storm. People are flocking to invest in them, at times without proper investigation and awareness of the possible pitfalls and scams.

The rush and the hype around bitcoin has attracted many hackers and scammers who are having a great time in the absence of a centralized authority handling the area. There are stories all over the media highlighting people who have made millions from them. Naturally people have flocked towards the new fad. Some of them completely unaware and most importantly unprepared for the dangers that lie ahead. Dangers in the form of scams and frauds that are just as real as the success stories. Bitcoin frauds and scams have become commonplace given the hype created around it. Scammers and fraudsters are having a hay day in the crypto-world because people are uninformed about their techniques. To exploit innocent folk, these cyber criminals have come up with elaborate schemes and fake coins that will make them rich at your expense

While the massive influx of the people and the interest that it has geared has developed a new industry, at the same time, it has also enabled leeches and scammers of the cyber world to benefit as much as possible. The only way to remain safe is to educate yourself about the nature of these crypto scams and how some of these operate. We will look at some common types of scammers and how they operate so that you can be better equipped at identifying them. How does one navigate the crypto bitcoin landscape without being scammed conned or hacked?

The frauds and scams are there along with the success stories. The scammers are having a field day with the amount of uninformed people they have at their disposal to play with. They are fully prepared and the main difference between them and us is they know what they are doing. They know the craft and they are experts. Unlike the some of the innocent people who just ended up in this world because they saw the trend and followed it.

The best way to steer clear of these people and their schemes is to educate yourself about what you are getting into and how do you play the game. Inform yourself about who these guys are? How do they operate? What scheme they come up with? And what are they doing now? Are they planning anything unique? Have they devised something new to trick you?

In this world of constant flux and new ambitious scammers you need to educate yourself and constantly stay on your toes. Read about them. Being informed is the best thing you can do.

And informing you is what we are going to do! Read this short ebook for some basic guidance about bitcoin and crypto scams and how to avoid them.

What is Bitcoin?

First of all, let's try to understand what bitcoin is and start with a little introduction to bitcoin. Satoshi Nakamoto published the original Bitcoin white paper in 2008 and 2009 saw its basic implementation.

This is a screenshot of the original Satoshi Nakamoto paper on Bitcoin.

Bitcoin: A Peer-to-Peer Electronic Cash System

Satoshi Nakamoto
satoshin@gmx.com
www.bitcoin.org

Abstract. A purely peer-to-peer version of electronic cash would allow online payments to be sent directly from one party to another without going through a financial institution. Digital signatures provide part of the solution, but the main benefits are lost if a trusted third party is still required to prevent double-spending. We propose a solution to the double-spending problem using a peer-to-peer network. The network timestamps transactions by hashing them into an ongoing chain of hash-based proof-of-work, forming a record that cannot be changed without redoing the proof-of-work. The longest chain not only serves as proof of the sequence of events witnessed, but proof that it came from the largest pool of CPU power. As long as a majority of CPU power is controlled by nodes that are not cooperating to attack the network, they'll generate the longest chain and outpace attackers. The network itself requires minimal structure. Messages are broadcast on a best effort basis, and nodes can leave and rejoin the network at will, accepting the longest proof-of-work chain as proof of what happened while they were gone.

1. Introduction

Commerce on the Internet has come to rely almost exclusively on financial institutions serving as trusted third parties to process electronic payments. While the system works well enough for most transactions, it still suffers from the inherent weaknesses of the trust based model. Completely non-reversible transactions are not really possible, since financial institutions cannot avoid mediating disputes. The cost of mediation increases transaction costs, limiting the minimum practical transaction size and cutting off the possibility for small casual transactions, and there is a broader cost in the loss of ability to make non-reversible payments for non-reversible services. With the possibility of reversal, the need for trust spreads. Merchants must be wary of their customers, hassling them for more information than they would otherwise need. A certain percentage of fraud is accepted as unavoidable. These costs and payment uncertainties can be avoided in person by using physical currency, but no mechanism exists to make payments over a communications channel without a trusted party.

What is needed is an electronic payment system based on cryptographic proof instead of trust, allowing any two willing parties to transact directly with each other without the need for a trusted third party. Transactions that are computationally impractical to reverse would protect sellers from fraud, and routine escrow mechanisms could easily be implemented to protect buyers. In this paper, we propose a solution to the double-spending problem using a peer-to-peer distributed timestamp server to generate computational proof of the chronological order of transactions. The system is secure as long as honest nodes collectively control more CPU power than any cooperating group of attacker nodes.

A Bitcoin is a digital number created by a mathematical function called a "HASH". It is accessed through a "public" and a "private" key. The quality which attracted the interest was that it is decentralized. It is held in a block chain which is a digital ledger. And the ledger is not kept in any one location but many.

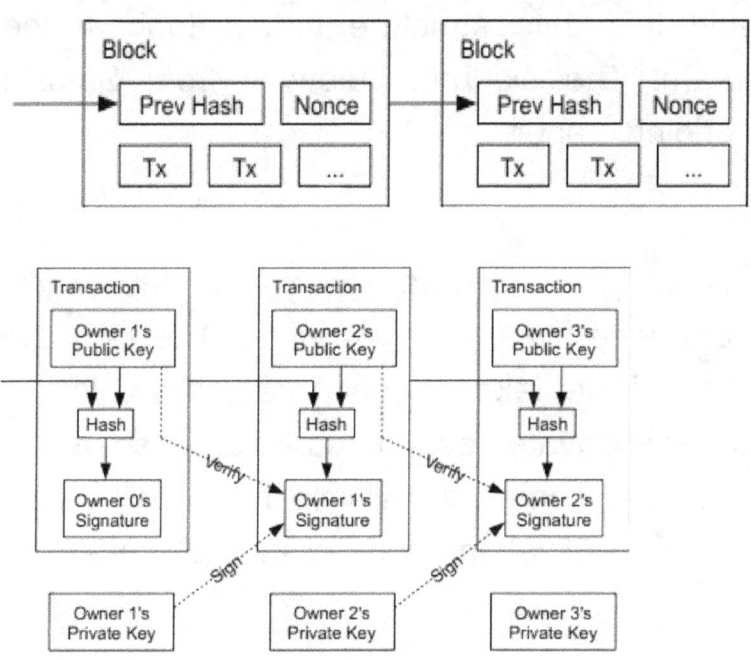

Source: Satoshi Nakamoto's Bitcoin whitepaper

Nakamoto talked about

- *Proof of Work: Random node in the network selects the next block to be added.*
- *Other nodes choose to either reject or accept that block: Validity of transactions (unspent, signed) comes into play*

6

- *Incentives for proof of work: Block reward, transaction fees.*
- *Forking possible: Only the blocks in the longest chain will be accepted by the majority, typically*

On the ledger, you can only add a new transaction. An existing transaction line cannot be modified or changed. To understand this data structure further look at the following digram. The diagram below is from Satoshi Nakamoto's original paper.

Every user is allotted a private key and a public key. These keys are generated by an algorithm. The keys are linked together. If we take a public key, it's going to generate a specific private key. The sure has to share the public key which is sometimes visible to all the users, which helps in verification and giving a sense of belonging.

Now the keys are always corresponding, so the public key which is more visible as compared to private key, may give hints of private keys to anyone looking for access to a private key. Now that, combined with further information about the private key user may be something to worry about for the key holder.

Satoshi Nakamoto, who has chosen to be anonymous for reasons unknown, developed the entity known as crypto currency. The quality that made people to gravitate towards it was it was decentralized and not controlled from one source. As a result, it stripped away the power anyone might have had had it been controlled by one source.

Nakamoto's Blockchain

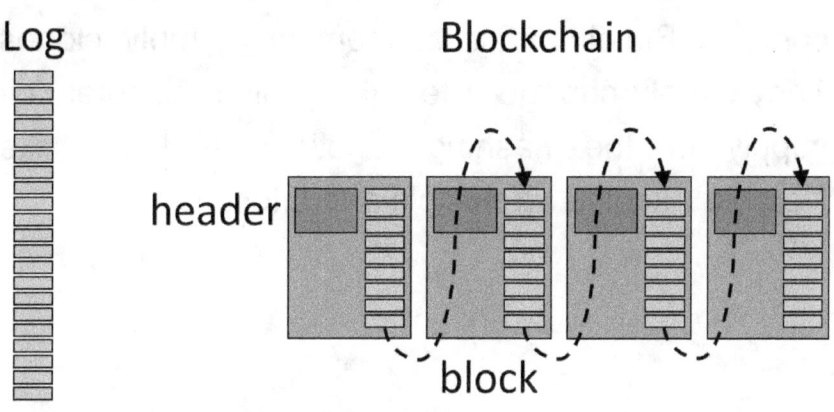

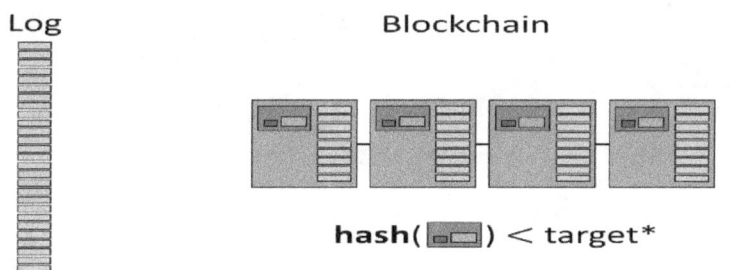

* *target*: a deterministic function of previous blocks

Source: Marco Canini

web.kaust.edu.sa/Faculty/MarcoCanini/classes/CS394B/S18/docs/L1-intro.pptx

- **The success of bitcoin naturally attracted other players in the market who came up with their own versions of digital coins**. Hence many alt coins were born. Now there are well over "alternate" coins to Bitcoin. 99% of them are simply clones. They simply change a few things like the total coin supply or the hashing functions and the like. Notable Altcoins are Ripple and Litecoin.

Phishing scams

Phishing is the illegal act of obtaining sensitive confidential details such as username or passwords through camouflaging websites etc. Users are fooled into thinking they are entering the information on a trusted website or a link that has been shared with them through emails or Google ads. What happens is that users are sent an email giving them the false idea that something has happened to their account or wallet and that they need to make it right by following a link. The link directs to a fake website, mostly resembling the original website with the same design and color schemes and font style forcing the visitors to think they are at the right place.

Once the user enters the information, it is then passed onto the scammers, who then use it the way they want to. They can use the information straight away or store it for later use depending upon the upside potential.

Myetherwallet is a prime example of this style of scams. A fake website was designed with the same design and look as the official website, hence making the users to provide the information as they would on the original platform. This resulted in huge losses to the users.

To think that the fake Myetherwallet app became one of the top 3 apps on the app store is scary. How easily it spread and affected so many users shows how vulnerable this industry can be as a result how vulnerable and prone to attacks users can be.

Another method is the use of airdrops. It's when fake companies pretend to be legitimate ones offer free tokens to a large number of people. Along them comes the need to download some app or a portal which is created by the same individuals looking to make easy money at your expense. They are required to enter the password and the usernames, exposing the private and the public keys as a result which enables the draining of the accounts.

How to avoid being scammed?

Now the question is what needs to be done to avoid such activities. The answer to that is be informed. Keep yourself up to date. The more we know about what's happening around the world, the better.

Subscribe to news and read as much as possible. Keep yourself informed. Discuss with people who know about the subject and talk about it. **It requires effort on your part.** Be curious. Know more.

The few things to keep in mind are as follows:

1. Make sure the website address you are visiting in such a situation is what you always see. Usually a few little differences are ignored or are hard to notice. But this is your hard earned money we are talking about here. So you have to be careful every single time you are asked to enter your details. Double check the address.
2. It has to start with "https" and not just "http".
3. Go with the gut feeling: If the website doesn't feel right, something looks off or there is something that feels different than routine. STOP! Do NOT proceed without verifying! Call a friend who knows a thing or two. Do something! Just don't go with flow.
4. Another very common tactic these fishy websites use is that use the sense of urgency. They give warnings. They use deadlines. They force the user to take an action as quickly as possible with big bold red titles with the text "HURRY" flashing like a traffic signal inciting panic and emergency in the minds. This forces the users to take a quick action without

thinking rationally and 99 times out of 100, the result of that is terrible.

5. Always set a strong password.
6. More importantly, REMEMBER that password. It is very common that people forget the passwords and they cannot access their own wallets.

Later on, we will explain in detail how to avoid scams and the Dos and Don'ts

Mining Scams

Mining scams are another interesting aspect of the scams. They use cloud mining. Now, not all cloud mining is illegitimate. Some use cloud mining for legitimate purposes. But like always, there are a few who have used cloud mining negatively and have carried out elaborate schemes to scam people.

Cloud mining is the process of mining bitcoins via a cloud. Here are companies that let people open an account with them and in return they let the users participate in the process of mining. The process is conducted on a cloud, hence eliminating the cost of equipment maintenance and energy.

There are some out there offering completely legitimate operations and there are people being a part of it. But at the same time, there are companies out there that are totally on the wrong side of the law and ethical boundary. THE RETURNS ARE one way of looking at these operations and judging either they are going to sting you or not. If the returns seem profitable, there is a chance it's totally fine and there is nothing to worry about. But if there are no or very minimal returns then that's a red flag. Steer clear of such setups. They aren't for you. Or anyone, for that matter.

Is the setup allowing a free scrutiny of the way they work, what tools they utilize and how are they planning to take the business forward, then you should be pretty sure that there is something that they do not want you or anyone outside of the inner circle to know. Transparency is very important. Every user has the right to know everything about the company they are going to be involved with. There should be no question about it.

Malware Scams

A malware portal is used to infect your pc and it hits right where it needs to in your space. Malicious software is created. Now once the computer is infected, the virus takes over and it can operate and take out the private information or data in a way it was designed to do.

There are numerous ways through which the job can be done.

An example is that that it can compromise your BTC wallet. When you attempt to send some coins to a friend in need, the original address may be replaced and with a fake one that belongs to the scammer.

A type of malware scam saw itself get noticed was called the Crypto Currency Clipboard Hijackers. They used the Windows clipboard as the weapon. Now some of these scammers used to use the windows clipboard to monitor a few thousand cyrptocurrency addresses but this one was pretty big. This one that was reported by some leading news portals used to monitor some 2.3 million addresses.

They use the copy paste mechanism of the Windows systems. As the addresses are usually long and difficult to remember, when the users used to copy and paste the addresses, that's when the scammers would replace the addresses with the forged ones. And the transactions would land in the wrong hands.

Here's how to spot such an activity

- Your pc slows signs of slowing down
- The pop ads, well they just pop up but there are too many to the point they begin to annoy
- You also may notice some unusual activity that you weren't responsible for

Fake Wallets

Scam	Lifetime		Payout to scammer	
	Days	Alive?	BTC	USD
Scam wallets	535	yes	4 105	$359 902
Scam exchanges				
BTC Promo	98	yes	44	$22 112
btcQuick		no	929	$73 218
CoinOpend	29	no	575	$264 466
Ubitex	91	no	30	$96[16]
Mining scams	Data Source			
Labcoin	Blockchain		241	$48 562
AMC	BitFunder		18 041	$1 327 590
Ice Drill	BitFunder		14 426	$1 558 008
Asic Mining	Blockchain		12.6	$5 532
Dragon Miner	Blockchain		1.63	$1 019

Vasek & Moore, Financial Crypto 2015: https://tylermoore.utulsa.edu/fc15.pdf

Fake wallets are also a favorite of scammers. They create a fake wallet to trick people to reveal their passwords and keys. Bitcoin gold was new to the market, and users who were looking to stake a claim were led on a fake wallet that went by the name of "mybtgwallet.com". Thinking this was the real thing; users provided their information regarding their private keys. And were deprived of millions of dollars as a result.

This scam emptied pockets and cost the users a combined amount that nears $3.5 million

Keeping in mind the amount of fake Google ads and advertisements being thrown at you every single day, you have to be very careful when visiting a website. The ideal thing to do is to just keep the original website that you use as bookmarked or type the address manually in your browser.

Here's how to spot such a scam

- The information about the model is not there
- There is no presence of it on big media outlets usually covering every aspect of this world
- The platform has been newly formed
- You don't see "Https". Instead there's just "Http"(meaning the connection isn't secure)

ICO SCAMS

ICO is an Initial coin offering that the developers or the creators conduct to raise money for their company or the startup. Since the main reason to conduct ICOs is to raise money, now the motive behind the money raising activity is what's important. It may differ sometimes. Some groups conduct ICOs and they are serious about what they are going to do with the money.

Since the money is raised, and there is no regulatory body to keep a check on the creators what they choose to do with the money, they are free to decide what happens and what doesn't. They can simply vanish onto thin air with the money or they can go the other direction and work within the legal confines.

A study conducted by the Wall Street Journal states that 1 in 5 Initial Coin Offerings [ICO] shows hints of fraudulent activates. That's 18.6%. That's a big chunk of the total ICOs conducted and it did have an impact on the market. Somewhere, somehow people were attached and involved in any capacity with these ICOs conducted.

ICOs are carried out to bypass the arduous process of finding capital investment through banks or VC capitalism. There is a massive surge in the amounts being raised by ICOs in the year 2018. The first 5 months of the year 2018 doubled the total of last year's total.

This trend shows that the bigger this segment of the crypto currency world gets, the chances of it getting affected by the scammers and fraudsters is likely to get higher.

A Prime example of an ICO scam is the Giza Scam. Almost $2 million were looted.

The project showed signs of warnings when the main supplier, which was supposed to develop their device, announced it had cut ties with Giza, citing reasons that were alarming for the audience. They alleged that the project seemed to be a scam. And they weren't in cooperation any more.

The supplier company, The Third Pin, who's CEO Ivan Larionov announced on a bit coin forum that his company has decided to cut ties with Giza. The explanation was as simple as that the Giza Honcho, known as Marco Fike, was unable to be clear throughout the negotiations and that was a major red flag. Referencing a particular point in time during the whole process, he specifically said that when inquired about when the device was supposed to roll out, Marco Fike, failed to describe what he wanted to do and what his plan was. It clearly indicated that the plan suggested publicly hadn't been worked out properly because the intention wasn't there at all. There was no seriousness and sincerity behind all the façade.

That's when the sole supplier decided to part ways with Giza. And this was the first blow in a series of many.

Soon after, the accounts began to dry up. Amounts had been transferred to other addresses.

Pump and Dump Scam

Pump and dump scams involve fake projection and showing promise and potential in an otherwise dead entity. This happens on a large scale. They scammers convince the buyers to invest and when the price reaches a tipping point, the projectors would dump the digital coins and eventually the market around it crashes. Because the potential wasn't there in the first place. It was a dead entity.

Pump and dump scams in the cyrptocurrency world are similar. The investors, some of whom aren't even willing to invest, are shown good promise and are led into believing that soon a major player would invest or partner up with the proposed entity and they are led into investing in it in an otherwise lifeless prospect. The rush caused by the believers then raises the price to a certain point and when the surge has maxed out, meaning it cannot go any further, which is understood by checking the volume that was estimated by the swindlers, the dumping starts. And soon, sometimes in a matter of minutes, the surge crashes, its short lived as expected.

This act is caused for a very simple reason. **Offloading! The market is manipulated in a way to minimize the losses of offloading**. And not just minimize the losses, most of the times a profit is scored on the expense people who are left with no choice but to grieve. What hits more is when the people realize they have been a part of an illegal activity without even knowing. Their involvement and buying power caused the price to go up, and when it went up, it came crashing down without a warning. Leaving no time to make a decision or get out. When the realization sets in, it's all over. As mentioned before, this scenario can play out in a matter of minutes. Rather than days or weeks.

Ponzi Schemes

These types of scams are exactly what the name suggests. We have all heard about how the Ponzi works. This classic scam technique is being used by traditional scammers who just can't get enough of their underhanded tactics. Very quickly they invaded the cyrptocurrency landscape and put the world on notice.

Ponzi schemes are schemes that take money from you, promising to multiply it, which they do sometimes by asking you to refer colleagues and family. The second tier influx brings about the capital to return the wealth of those who came first. The newer investors however are rarely lucky when it comes to wealth being returned, multiplied because by then the scheme has been stopped on accounts of fraud and deceit. Did I mention that investment is done on a non-existent entity? Which means there wasn't any mechanism in the first place to multiply wealth other than grabbing money from the later investors who have been referred to them, by YOU?

Sounds nice and warm!

These schemes run as long as the cat isn't out of the bag. The sooner the investors find out somehow, that they have been investing in a property, or product that does not exist anywhere in the world, they first action is to demand a return. Which obviously never goes smoothly? By now, it's already too late. Most of the money has been transported to foreign lands, laundered, or been used to fund any illegal activities, or it can be anywhere in the world. It doesn't matter where the money is or how it's been used, what matters is by then, people have been ripped off. The extent of the damage inflicted can be measured but the effect it had, cannot.

How to Spot a Ponzi scam

- The revenue is exponentially high
- The success is dependent on referrals
- The business model feels incomplete

- Lack of transparency and lack of information of the company and the team behind it

These indicators are usually not very hard to find. If one may look with a keen eye and just a little bit of effort on your part may expose a scheme before it's too late.

Real Life scams examples

Here's a list of real life scams. There is a chance that reading about these scams may give you jitters and somehow you will be discouraged to get into if there was a plan in the first place to be a part of this phenomenon. But remember, this eBook is just to give you a basic idea of how it happens, when it happened and why it happened and what were the repercussions. I had to go back and forth and decide whether to include these in my write up. Because reading about so many scams, and some of these are huge in volume and the amount of damage they left in their trail. Reading all the negative stuff associated about one thing that has happened in the same place may put doubts in the minds of the potential investors. It's a fact that when a person hears all about the warning stuff sporadically from different sources that has a more solid and a more positive effect in the sense that a receiver doesn't panic. They take the information one by one, which helps in maintaining the pace of the mind. As a result, the decision making also takes place at an effective and therapeutic pace. You can call this more of a slow penetration approach. Whereas an article or an n eBook in this case, decides to put all the stuff in the same place, it may have an effect of panic and chaos and paranoia. But be assured, this eBook is just for the purpose of educating the readers. There might be such people, who are planning right now to jump, then there might be a group who is past the stage of planning and just waiting for that last little push that will make them take the step; I hope this eBook arrives on their desktops, laptops or pads just in time. So that before they proceed, they have a look at this and analyze if they have really prepared themselves for this wild and unhinged world of crypto currencies.

So where we go:

Plexcoin

Dominic Lacroix, the founder of Plexcoin was jailed for conducting a fraud ICO, raising close to $15 million from thousands of investors. Lacroix, whose activities had already caught the attention of the regulatory authorities even before the ICO, was ordered to not proceed with the fundraising. He decided to move ahead paying no attention. His rebellious act attracted a contempt of court charge and a two month jail sentence. On top of that, he and his company DL Innov were slapped with a $110,000 fine.

He appeared before court and was asked to transfer the funds. Upon the request, he complied.

Bitconnect

Divyesh Darji, alleged to be one of the key people behind the Bitconnect scam, was arrested in Dubai this year. The allegation that Bitconnect ripped off roughly $15 million from the investors was enough for Gujarat Criminal Investigation Department (CID) to take the step.

The company was registered in the UK and was headquartered in Surat. They ran a promotion campaign on social media, held parties all over the world to get the attention it wanted. The tagline was "60% monthly interest" which sounded pretty sweet to all those willing investors. At its peak, the price of BCC was $363.62 and now it stands at $0.67. After having the operations shut down citing bad press and US regulatory scrutiny as reasons.

OneCoin

OneCoin has been officially labeled as a Ponzi scheme in India. The company claimed to have been registered in Vietnam but the country later refuted the claims. Various scandals over the world in different countries proved that OneCoin indeed was a scam.

Thailand, Croatia, Bulgaria, Finland and Norway warned the investors of the potential risks involved regarding the company.

In 2016, over $30 million were seized by the Chinese government when they decided to look into the matter.

CentraTech

CentraTech is another name in the long list of scams. The founders raised close to $32 million in an ICO conducted last year. Why it makes the list here is because huge names from the popular culture such as Floyd Mayweather and DJ Khaled. It was very important that we mention this high profile case because of the amount of hype that surrounded it initially. The marketing went into overdrive acquiring A-liters to the bidding. Now that was a first for a cyrptocurrency. Obviously the fame and believability came along with names. Riding the coattails was a simple yet highly effective strategy that paid off very nicely in the form of big dough coming in.

Convincing the investors is one of the major objectives in any business and with big names on their side, half the job was done.

Personally, the monetary volume in the scam seems a bit less considering how easy it was for them. But maybe we will never know why they stopped at the amount at which they did.

The team is looking at a 65 year prison sentence.

A list of now blacklisted crypto currencies

Here is a brief list of some crypto currencies that have either been blacklisted or are close to being one of the many.

2xbits.blogspot.com

Yourbitcoinbanker.com

bitconnect.co

Activebitcoinminers.com

Bitcoin-manager.info

Genuinebitcoinmultiplier.com

Bitwallio.com

bitcashworld.com

Cryptofly.net

Iseiko.jp

Fastpaybtc.com

Here is a list of some names that are more likely to be Ponzi schemes than genuine entities

1. BCC Cash (note that this is different from Bitcoin Cash)
- BCHconnect
- Billion Bit Club
- Binary Coin
- Bit Sequence

- BitAI
- Bitchamps
- Bitclub/clubcoin
- Bitcoin Ascension (pyramid scheme)
- Bitconnect X
- Bitether
- Bitfinite
- Bitfintech
- Bitglare Coin
- Btchash
- Btc-Rush
- Btcwait
- Chrysos
- Coinrium
- Cointeum
- Coinspace
- Dascoin
- Ecomcash
- Eigencoin
- ETHconnect
- Etherbanking
- Exacoin
- Falcon Coin
- Farstcoin
- Ficoin
- Firstcoin
- Forzacoin
- Futurecoin
- FUU Coin
- Gold Reward Token
- Goldgate
- Hedgeconnect
- Hextracoin
- Home Block Coin
- HotCrypto

- Hydrocoin
- Ibiscoin
- iCenter
- Ideacoin
- iFan
- Iotaconnect
- Knox Coin
- Legendcoin
- Lendconnect
- Lendera
- Libra Coin
- Liteconnect
- Loancoin
- Martcoin
- Moneroconnect
- Monetize Coin
- Monyx
- Neoconnect
- Numiv
- Oalend Coin
- Onecoin
- Pagarex
- Purpose/DUBI
- Regalcoin
- Rothscoin
- Secular Coin
- SFICoin
- Steneum
- Stepium (pyramid scheme)
- Swisscoin (pyramid scheme)
- Tenocoin
- TEX Coin
- Thorn Coin
- Ucoin Cash
- Unix Coin

- USI Tech
- WCI
- Western Coin
- XRPconnect

Defunct ponzi schemes:

1. Ambis
- Bitcoinly
- Bitconnect
- Bithaul
- Bitlake
- Bitpetite
- Bitsupreme
- Btcbox.cc
- Chain.Group
- Coinreum
- Control Finance
- Cryptodouble
- Davor
- Ethtrade
- Laser Online
- LoopX
- Mavro
- Mecoin
- Metizer
- Microhash
- Paycoin
- Plexcoin
- Thunderbit
- Vixice
- Vone

How to steer Clear of such Scams

There are always red flags. Sometimes they are too prominent to spot and sometimes they aren't. But surprisingly, glaring red flags aren't enough to stop the people. Casual investor, who are not in it for the long haul and are just following a fad, or doing it out curiosity, they fall prey. Similarly, the businesses with the not so glaring red flags also make money and prey on those who are smarter than the casual investor. So it seems everyone in the scamming world has their share cut out for them. It seems scamming, as prevalent as it is in crypto currency world is relatively easy. And that's true to some extent. Because as long as there are people out there who aren't willing to put in the work and effort to know as much as possible about these scams, there will always be someone to take advantage of this behavior.

Below we have compiled a list of things to look out for when you decide to get into crypto currency. The below mentioned points can be made into a sort of checklist and saved onto your computer or mobile phone. So whenever there is a social media post, or an email, or a link plastered all over the internet that compels you to invest and it sounds to too good to be true. At least you will have the checklist. If there are red flags you need to stop.

So here we go

Public profile

If the creators are promising a public repository, then there has to be one. It simply cannot be any other way. Without a front, a face that seems legitimate, there is no guarantee that the team or the setup actually exists. There is no proof they have a plan to work on, there is no guarantee that they even have a tech team working on the product. It can all be just eye wash and there is no better way to say otherwise than to see it.

Zero Activity

If there is no activity for longer time periods, it signals that something is wrong. Most Crypto currencies launch and start with the promise of tremendous of growth. The hype is created by marketing, referrals, and sweeping statements, but they fizzle out. That means they didn't have the staying power or the persistence to keep going. And as a result, the lack of activity starts to show. The lack is a major signal that the future is bleak and that being a part of this process can hardly be worthwhile. It's nearly impossible for a company to start again and climb when once it has fizzled out, the word of mouth has spread and there is a bad impressing among the investors. So a company that's slowing down, almost to a halt, rarely ever gets back up again. And you need to stay away from such establishments]

Small team

Its common knowledge that for anything to take off, a group of passionate individuals, working together professionally, is needed. A one man show, sooner or later, crashes when the popularity soars high. So the bigger the team, the better, It shows the company has successfully been able to define roles to certain individuals. It also projects commitment that the company is here to stay for the long haul.

No advisers

Advisors are an important asset to the company. Advisors make the team stay afloat when the going gets tough. Those who are responsible for the daily grind, when they are down and out, that's when the advisors step up and they steer the ship in the right direction. So the presence if an adviser or many, reassures the commitment and shows seriousness to the cause.

No diversity

As mentioned before, a large team has more chances of succeeding than a small one. Practically speaking! When the roles are defined, and there is a person for job, it keeps things smooth and streamlined. Just a group of tech geeks won't cut it. A company needs people with different skill set to make it big. Marketers, engineers, designers, coordinators are all equally vital if the company aims go big.

Anonymous team

There was a time when anonymity was a matter of pride in the crypto currency world. People used to behave a certain way, possibly because the creator of bit coin himself, who is almost worth $700million, has chosen to remain anonymous to this day. But that was then. Now that the industry has grown so much and has turned into a giant of sorts, anonymity now means suspicion. It's high time this industry starts acting like a mature industry. This has to change. Can we imagine a world where in automobile industry the chairman of Ford motors chooses to not be seen by anyone and hides in the shadows? No! It's high time the industry evolves and it is evolving, thankfully. It needs to operate like any other normal industry with people who have public profiles and presence

No team engagement

The team should be able to interact with the world they have decided to be a part of. Attending conferences, marking their presence, making the world know they are here and putting in the effort to blend in. this is a very positive behavior that makes everyone believe that they are here to stay and they have nothing to hide from the rest of the world. Just imagine that your next door neighbor who is mysterious and doesn't talk to anyone in the street. Even if he is a good guy, people talk in hushed tones and suspect that there is something to worry about even when there isn't.

Exposed infighting

When the team isn't really well knit together, and it shows. Sometimes it spills over right in front of the public eye. This signals that the end is near. Bad publicity is something that hardly anyone recovers from. Imagine the opposite, all posing together and posing for photographs on vacations. Would that be a sight to see and instill warmth in the eyes of the observer or would fighting be preferred?

No funding

A lot of the times what happens is that funds start to dry up and there is nothing left for the team that can make them stick to the cause and work towards betterment and completion. Majority is in it for the money. Very few are in it for the love of the craft. When the worldly gains are no longer there to be benefitted from, the teams usually split and the goal that once was the mainstay takes a back seat and eventually disappears in the background. Resulting in shutting down of the whole operation. A check on funding will help interested people to make sure that the company has the resources to stay here and it won't be packing up as soon as the empty accounts start to pop up.

Mystery funding

Transparency in this regard is of utmost importance. Often times companies claim one thing about the funding's and when they are corrected by someone outside of the group, it creates for an embarrassing situation. Branding the team as frauds falsifying information in this aspect is ridiculous at this point because a funding source can be easily verified. When the information initially given turn s out to be false, there is little anyone can do to regain the trust of the people.

A lack of a white paper.

A white paper has been integral to many new startups in the recent years. It is published at the very beginning to outline the company plans regarding the future covering major aspects such as the vision behind the idea, the motivation, and how much better the idea is going to make the global landscape of the crypto currency. The more detailed it is, the better it is for the investors and the creators. After all it is usually the first impression, so it better be good. So when a white paper is missing, its considered a bad sign and the investors gets the idea that maybe there is a lack of direction or the creators haven't really figured out what they ate going to do or how they are bring about a big change. It shows lack of maturity and lack planning on the part of creators.

Plagiarized white paper

Is it even worth talking about? I mean do I need to say more? Who does that?

Lack of technical details in the white paper

The method with which the vision is supposed to be executed has to be in the paper. Remember! You cannot take white paper and not give it its due importance. It shows the amount of hard work and brainstorming that has gone into the building of the idea from the ground up. A white paper that is not taken seriously and the creators, for some reason decide to not include an elaborate plan make a big mistake. Anyone user who decides to jump on the bandwagon need to look for these red flags and make the best of decisions based on the findings.

Lack of a timeline

A team that does not specify the time limit shows that it lacks the confidence to implement the vision. Meaning there is still room for a lot of work and homework needs to be done. It also shows that they have probably published the white paper a little too prematurely. And the development still hasn't matured enough to be considered a viable contender to make it in the space.

Marketing in overdrive

Marketing is usually done to the peak in this arena. And sometimes too much marketing casts a negative impact on the actual product. This is true for every product in the world whether it's in the crypto world or anywhere else. The product often doesn't live up to the hype and in turn disappoints the user. Another common practice that is rampant is that marketing is usually done for a project that is still in development stages and hasn't matured yet. It's just hype. So when a coin starts to skyrocket, make investigations why it is happening. Is it just marketing that's causing it to shoot or is there is any substance behind it? If it's just marketing, instability can be expected in the future.

False marketing

Often cases spring up, where there are false claims at play. As mentioned before, some projects still haven't took off and they are marketing features that are still in theory and are proposed ideas. That doesn't mean they will be a part of final product that rolls out.

Tall claims

When there are tall claims, they have to be backed up by substantial proof and a proper roadmap that highlights each and every step that needs to be taken. It has to be solid as hell. When someone reads, there shouldn't be a hint of hollowness or hockey stuff.

Publicity stunts that fall flat

More and more people rely on stunts that usually fall flat and don't really serve a purpose. They focus more on partnerships with big names, flashy events being organized but through all of that stuff, its serves no purpose. It feels useless in the long run. After all how fruitful can these stunts be when there are major loopholes in the functionality of the product itself.

Currency viability

Most of the coins in the market are specific to certain group of people. It is very easy to capture a niche market, because most coins have been doing that since the beginning. A more general coin is needed. People don't want to switch among a few dozen coins every now and then to buy different things.

Need

Does the coin serve a purpose? Does the coin need to exist? If the coin disappears the very next day will it affect the market the users in anyway? Will the users be deprived of some vital function or service? The answers to these questions justify the need of the coin? If the coin does not serve a purpose then it doesn't need to be here in the first place.

Complexity

There is already too much to handle in the world. If the existence of a particular coin doesn't simplify the things and rather over complicate things, then that's not going to play well in the long run. Sooner or later, it's going to get discarded.

Ponzi schemes

If the plan regarding a Ponzi scheme resembles that of a Ponzi scheme, then chances are it is one. There are no guaranteed returns. When a coin is marketed as a sure shot success, chances are that it is going to bring a lot of disappointment in the future. And it is best to steer clear.

Distribution of funds

There is sort of a tradition that the tokens from ICO are allocated to the team itself. Now the amount allocated is what we are pointing out. A 5% allocation does make sense. A 20% plus allocation is highly unreasonable. This raises eyebrows as the investors may question the logic behind such an unorthodox approach.

Conclusion

Here is the deal. There are a lot of red flags that can help you identify which ones having the potential and which ones do not. These have been presented here just to give you an idea of what is they. Behind these, there's no rocket science, if you looks close enough and observe just a little bit, these are easily noticeable and can easily be spotted. A list of all warning signs also makes it easier in the sense that, if you can make a checklist of these, scrutiny will be made easy and you won't need to go to different places and forums to get the idea about a certain crypto currency.

In the end, I would like to share a transcript from a workshop hosted by Federal Trade Commission. Reading this, you will feel like there's some practical activity in the government corridors to prevent scams, how to identify them, what are the future plans and how to tackle the issue.

There's a genuine effort in this regard. Also there's always room for improvement. It's a simple cycle. No matter what steps we take, the scammers usually find a way to overcome them. And that's what has been happening since the start of time. We have to realize that this will continue to happen.

It's going to go on and on forever. The best we can do is to "minimize" these illegal fraudulent activities. We cannot stop it completely. We can limit them. That's all we can do.

One very last important point is that the best way to minimize scams in cyrptocurrency is to educate yourself.

Bad guys don't win because they are perfect at their jobs.

Bad guys win because the good guys were too lazy to do a good job.

The good guys were too careless. The good guys give an opening and that's when the bad guys hit and they hit hard. Because let's face it, the amount of ambitious bad guys is much more than ambitious good guys.

So here it is.

FTC Decrypting Cryptocurrency Scams Workshop

June 25, 2018

Transcript

"..And so to go through the list, you'll hear a lot of these things are very similar to the kind of scams that you've seen from the early days of the internet.So one example being an exit scam. The most recent one that I know of was by Confito, and it was for $375,000. And essentially Confito had offered a decentralized escrow project. And pretty much within overnight, there was a big legal problem for why Confito had to shut down and they walked away with $375,000 of investor money. They had a legitimate looking web site. They had a legitimate looking white paper. And they basically, you know, created a lot of hype and then were able to walk away. Bait and switch and impersonation is another really popular wayfor consumers to be scammed with initial coin offerings where a company will either pretend to be another reputable company, have like a similar URL address and maybe try to pretend to bethat other company."

"Or another thing is that they would have legitimate looking people on their web site, LinkedIn profiles, and actually be total frauds. One example of that was Benabit. They were offering a back loyalty program where if you invested, you would see great rewards from investing in this company. And they raised somewhere between-- well, I guess walked away with somewhere between $2.7 and $4 million. And the way that their scam came to light was someone noticed that the LinkedIn profiles of their founders were actually staff members at a UK boys' school who had nothing to do with the project."

You also see traditional Ponzi schemes where you're robbing from Peter to pay Paul, basically as new people come on the people who have been involved are getting the money at their returns from people who had already been-- or from the newer people. And as Andrew Smith talked about in the opening, you'll also see change or what I talked about with my grandmother, like pyramid schemes where everyone who is involved recruits more members. And as more members come in, there's a trickle up effect of that. And then there are ones that are not technological at all. They're just

42

phishing scams where you'll get-- A most recent example is Betoken. Betoken was essentially offering to be a new version of Airbnb. And you would buy the token that would give you some ownership in that company--not ownership...hackers sent out an email pretending to be Betoken. And they added this sense of urgency of, you know, if you buy now, Microsoft is going to participate in this deal. And they were able to get their login information and take about $833,000. And another kind of phishing scam is what's called an airdrop. And again, that is about a sense of urgency, where companies will offer either very low cost or free tokens to try to drive interest in the new projects. And what they'll do is they'll require you to download something or they'll require you to get a native wallet, like a wallet that they've created. And by doing that, they'll be able to access your public and private keys, and also take whatever tokens you put in there. And so it seems like a great deal because you're getting something for low value or free, but actually they're getting a lot of information out of you and your money.

And then the last one I'll talk about is a pump and dump, where you'll see online forums or other

groups of coordinated efforts to manipulate the value of a token. And so these groups move

together, try to drive interest in the token. The volatility and the price increase. And then as soon

as they all kind of hit a certain level, they all understand what it is, they will dump and they will

walk away with the money. And those other consumers coming in will be caught up in that.

There's probably more but that's what I've got for you.

My work has also looked at online scam wallets. So these are services that pretend to be a wallet.

They might hold your money, if you only have a small amount of money in it. But then once you

put a larger amount in, they'll take all of your money and run. One of the big hallmarks of these is that they're currently primarily only offered on the dark web

You have to think about all these other things that can get triggered when you're operating in this

environment. And we've done it not just for the US, but multiple countries. And we continue to

add to that. And I hope even once we've published this document, we'll continue to add more

countries to make it truly global. It's a ecosystem and you can't just-- you can't be myopic in how

you're looking at the law.

We need to be able to thoroughly investigate those cases and stop. If the ongoing conduct is

fraudulent and people are going to get hurt, we need to stop it right away.

About half of the Ponzi schemes we found died within a week of first being advertised. Some of these died

because they got no traction. Some of them got too much traction and couldn't actually pay out

when they said they would. And then about the other half last longer than that. These are usually

the other half that so-called investors look for.

And we also note that within things that last shorter than a week, a lot of these people that invest

in it are seeing this as some sort of like online gambling thing. So it's less of a Ponzi scheme

investment thing and more of a, like, hey, let's see if everybody else is going to participate in this

scheme and try to bring unity of our friends on the forum, and unity of everybody on Twitter, or whatever have you.So then talking about the work on coins, so there's been this proliferation of coins. We looked at,like, on the order of 1,200 different coins that were offered in the past three, four years. And

what we found is that some of them start at a good price because they had this big ICO beforehand. And then investors, a lot of times, will have to hold onto their money for a while. Sothe people who started the coin can get out first.

The investors, when they try to go out, there's all of this supply of coin. Nobody actually wants it

because they can't actually use it for anything, and so it just falls right down. And so what we can see is that what happened is back in 2015, around there, there was a lot of coins that were introduced and then just abandoned. And we've seen in the last year a big resurgence of these coins. So they died. They went away after their big skyrocket. They were trading at less than $1 for years, and then now we've seen them starting to trade again.The internet is a fantastic tool. You find all sorts of things on it. You know, that's how we're finding these fake pictures and these fake videos. You know, I hate to say it. I'd love to say we have some really secret law enforcement technique that we're able to use. You know, our law enforcement technique's called Google. Secret law enforcement technique, find the most technical language in the white paper, enter it in word for word, and see how many white papers pop up with the same language.

And then in December the complaints skyrocketed, and by March they fell again. Because that buzz around the skyrocketing price of Bitcoin did get a lot more people involved and active.

So in the state of Indiana and Massachusetts where we have homes, there are very robust counsels on aging that provide all kinds of services. I worry that vulnerable populations, people who don't speak English very well and are newly arrived, people who are at home a lot,vulnerable to the 15,000 telemarketing calls we all get every day but we're not there for, but they're there to answer the phone. They don't hear well. The English is sometimes accented

 Consumer Financial Protection Bureau has a great complaint database that you can lookat. But in this particular arena, it lumps remittance payments, wire transfers, and virtual currency problems into one category.And the most recent search I did preparing for this panel showed-- this was last week--approximately 6,800 complaints. But when you read them, many of them, the person being—the entity, rather, being complained about was a bank. So that is harder when you get down to the more granular level and you look at what the complaint actually is about, it may or may not have anything to do with virtual currency, to the degree that agencies can keep better-- keep and then publish better data.

Of course, for us to stay on top of how developments in technology are affecting consumers, it's critical for us to hear from them directly. If you or someone you know experiences a cryptocurrency scam, please file a complaint with the FTC at ftc.gov

www.ingramcontent.com/pod-product-compliance
Lightning Source LLC
Chambersburg PA
CBHW081621220526
45468CB00010B/2979